Lang Art Gallery
Scripps College, Claremont

November 9–December 21, 1977

Catalogue by David S. Rubin
Curated by Neda Al-Hilali and David S. Rubin

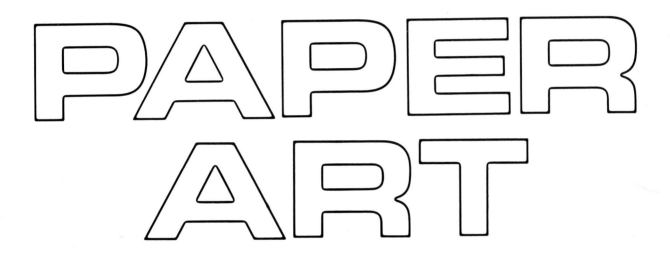

Galleries of the Claremont Colleges
Pomona College   Scripps College

Foreword

In the past three years the program of the Galleries of the Claremont Colleges has concentrated primarily on works on paper. Our most ambitious exhibitions have been ones of drawings, prints and photographs. It is therefore appropriate that Neda Al-Hilali and David S. Rubin have organized an exhibition of works *in* paper, particularly because it is in this medium that some of the most exciting developments in the visual arts today are taking place.

I would like to personally thank Neda Al-Hilali and David S. Rubin for all of their thought and effort which they so willingly and generously gave in organizing this splendid exhibition.
David W. Steadman,
Director

Acknowledgements

Organizing an exhibition in contemporary art requires a great deal of cooperation from artists and their dealers. We are extremely grateful to the following dealers, not only for their generous time and hospitality, but for their enthusiastic support of the exhibition: Abe Adler (Adler Gallery), Louise Allrich (The Allrich Gallery), Ruth Braunstein (Braunstein/Quay Gallery), Claire Copley (Claire S. Copley Gallery), Dede Coyle (Smith Andersen Gallery), Toni Danzig (Source Gallery), Steve Foster (ADI Gallery), Ursula Gropper (Grapestake Gallery), Donald Guild (Gemini G.E.L.), Paula Kirkeby (Smith Andersen Gallery), Jean Millant (Cirrus Gallery), Fay Ann Potter (William Sawyer Gallery), Victor Schiro (Gemini G.E.L.), Steve Sotnik (Vanguard Gallery) and also to Ann and Garner Tullis of the International Institute for Experimental Printmaking.

For inviting us to visit their studios we wish to thank Charles Christopher Hill and Jay McCafferty; Nancy Genn and Richard Royce were kind enough to speak with us at length about their work, as was Karen Laubhan. A very special thanks to Don Farnsworth for demonstrating the papermaking process at his workshop. *JP-Four Squares No. 1* (cat. no. 14) was made in my presence.

For opening their homes to us, a word of gratitude to collectors Morton and Jean Beckner, Charles and Terry Daugherty, and David and Cloyce Flaten.

I also wish to thank dealer Mitzi Landau and artist Tim App for their helpful suggestions on where to find new work.

Thank you to all the artists who generously responded to the questionnaire, thereby contributing important information to this catalogue. Ron McPhearson, who headed the Sonnier project for Gemini G.E.L. provided details about how the pieces were made. Roland Reiss furnished data on the works by David Smith.

The problems of accurate documentation were made so much easier through the willing assistance of Jeff Fraenkel (Grapestake Gallery), Noel Garin (ADI Gallery), Susan Ingram (Braunstein/Quay Gallery), Georgianna M. Lagoria (The Allrich Gallery), and Rita Olsen (Atelier Royce), and, of course, of the individual artists.

The catalogue could not have come together so swiftly without the diligent efforts of registrar Kay Koeninger Warren and photographer Neil Fenn.

I am grateful to David W. Steadman for his expert advice and guidance, and to Neda Al-Hilali for her impeccable judgment in co-selection of the exhibition.
David S. Rubin,
Assistant Director

Introduction

The "paper movement" of the 1970s has rapidly been finding its place in the history of art. Partly as a result of an increase in collaboration between artist and print workshops or paper mills,[1] many artists, from a variety of diverse backgrounds, have developed new methods of working with commercial paper, or making their own pulp and exploring the flexibility and numerous possibilities of manipulating it while wet. Paper no longer functions merely as a background surface, but rather, asserts itself as an integral part of a work's expression. As Susan E. Meyer noted recently, "Artists are finding that they can shape paper, cast it, laminate it, emboss it, dye it, glue it," and so on.[2] Richard Kubiak divides handmade papermaking techniques into four essential groups: "embedding, layering, modeling, and coloring," while also noting that "there are . . . as many combinations and variations as there are artists."[3]

The present exhibition demonstrates that whether the paper employed is made by the artist himself or comes from another source, similar results are sometimes obtained. Al-Hilali's *Althee* (1977; cat. no. 4), McCafferty's *Participation* (1977; cat. no. 38), and Genn's *Rain Bar Drawing* (1977; cat. no. 19) are all wall relief pieces with rugged edges and aggressive surface textures. Yet they vary in scale, degree of relief, format of compositional field, and method of construction. Al-Hilali and McCafferty used commercial paper. The former employed it as a weaving material, while the latter burned large gashes into it with a magnifying glass. Genn's piece was made by carefully laying out bands of paper which she manufactured herself.

One may find it instructive to organize the works in the exhibition into a number of dichotomies: large scale versus small scale, intimate versus powerful, two-dimensional versus three-dimensional, colorful versus textural, handmade paper versus commercial paper, and so forth. Clearly Charles Christopher Hill's *Black, Orange, Beige* (1972; cat. no. 23), Alexander's *Four Voices* (1976; cat. no. 3), and Sonnier's *R-VII* (1976; cat. no. 70) are all monumental in scale; yet the Hill piece was sewn together, the Alexander piece taped, and the Sonnier hand-shaped with molds. Of the three, only the Alexander is sculptural. In contrast to this group, Di Mare's *Spirit Bundle No. 1* (1977; cat. no. 10) and Royce's *Frozen Motion Series* (1977; cat. nos. 53–55) are so small that they must be placed on pedestals and viewed at close range. Attempting to categorize works in this fashion, then, should make one aware of the complexities involved,

since no uniform classification will work for a single artist. A comparison of Farnsworth and Clinton Hill will illustrate just how subtle are the differences that emerge. Both artists treat handmade paper pieces as a form of drawing or painting. Each incorporates brightly colored graphic imagery within the paper itself, keeping in the composition a clear separation between figure and ground. In *JP-Four Squares No. 1* (1977; cat. no. 14) Farnsworth drew directly into a freshly couched sheet of paper with his own mixture of dyed liquid pulp; pigments were avoided in order to prevent the colors from bleeding into the background. In contrast to this, Hill spooned pigments into *No. 52* (1975; cat. no. 25) with the intention of achieving that very result. While Farnsworth's configurations simulate the transluscency of watercolor, Hill's recall the bold broad brushstrokes of a Kline or DeKooning.

Perhaps the key to understanding paper art is in realizing that all of the artists are dealing, on some level, with a problem that has an extensive heritage in the history of art: the relation between content and form.

Art historians have been able to distinguish content from form in almost any period. "Content" usually refers to subject matter or, in conceptual art, the idea being put forth. "Form" designates the plastic properties within a work—line, shape, color, texture, etc. In the Renaissance paintings of Raphael, for example, content and form interact. Form usually aids in the expression of the meaning: placing three figures within a triangular shaped area was a common practice of Raphael, and helped to clarify the relationship among the figures. Certainly form contributed to meaning in Impressionist landscapes, where autonomous dabs of paint enlivened the picture surface and paralleled the feeling of real atmosphere.

In the twentieth century there has been a greater consciousness of the form/content relationship. In some instances form and content continue to be compatible within a single work. In others they have gone separate directions, so that one seems to overshadow the other. Formal problems were of little concern to Dali, whose Surrealist paintings use Renaissance space to create dream imagery. Mondrian's paintings are formalist in that his pictorial vocabulary is non-objective. But, as was the case with several of the first abstract painters, the straight lines and primary colors were intended to signify something; the balance and harmony of the composition was the equivalent of a philosophical idea of cultural equilibrium. Although form seemed primary, form and content were still compatible and distinguish-

3

able, but the nature of "content" had taken on a new dimension. In recent years many artists have isolated form to the point where it actually *becomes* the content. This is applicable to abstract studies in formal relationships where no concept or subject is present other than the expression of the material itself. Alber's paintings or Caro's sculptures are as formalist as can be. In the former the content is canvas and paint; it is steel I-Beams and paint in the latter.

How, then, do these principles apply to paper art? In short, paper allows artists to continue the twentieth century traditions cited above, but with an enormous amount of flexibility. Paper is a medium which lends itself quite easily to the formal or the conceptual. When the material carries the entire meaning, as is often the case in contemporary paper art, content and form are one and the same.

It should be remembered that paper was an important solution for Braque and Picasso when they sought to unify representation and abstraction in their mature Cubist paintings and drawings. The use of small pieces of paper as formal elements enabled them to do just that in their early collages and *papiers collés.* Braque's action of pasting a piece of ordinary wallpaper on to a drawing in 1912 is extremely significant historically when considered in light of present day uses of paper.[4] Braque was the first artist to use paper as anything other than a background surface.[5] This important gesture came directly from a desire to clarify subject matter and simultaneously assert the autonomy of the applied paper. Wallpaper with a simulated wood grain pattern was used to represent a wooden object, such as a table or chair. Aware that collage and *papier collé* made the surfaces of their drawings and paintings more tangible, Braque and Picasso began describing their medium as *"tableau-objet"* rather than using the conventional term *"tableau."* John Golding offers a succinct explanation of Braque's important contribution:

> The fragments of *papier collé* here can be said to exist on three levels. They are flat, coloured, pictorial shapes. They represent or suggest certain objects in the picture by analogies of colour and texture or by the addition of keys or clues. Thirdly, and this is the aspect of *papier collé* that most relates it to other forms of Cubist *collage,* the pieces of paper exist as themselves, that is to say one is always conscious of them as solid, tactile pieces of extraneous matter incorporated into the picture and emphasizing its material existence.[6]

Golding's first observation pertains to form and the second to content as subject. It is the third point, however, which suggests the possibility of content and form being the same.

In contemporary paper art, when a work is made entirely of paper, with no other medium used to embellish it, then the paper becomes the primary carrier of expression or meaning. In this way paper can easily function as form and content simultaneously. In contrast to *papier collé,* however, the bond between form and content can be displayed throughout the entire image rather than being restricted to its separate parts.

A majority of artists in the current exhibition do unify form and content into a single image. But most are also concerned with the concepts, ideas, or associations which stem from their use of an old material in a new way. The nature of the content, then, may be complex, operating on more than one level. In most of the formalist works, the content as paper is the chief or sole conveyor of formal relationships. But this is usually coupled with the expression of content on a conceptual level. There are also several artists in the exhibition who concern themselves more with content than with form. But even here paper is a necessary component in the communication of a feeling or idea.

Only three artists in the exhibition could be considered pure formalists. The work of Farnsworth, Genn, and Kinnee is about abstract shapes, colors, and forms. Farnsworth's method of forming an abstract composition within rather than on top of the paper has already been described. Genn's larger paper pieces have an impact similar to that found in 1960s colorfield painting. The broad vertical bands in *Uxmall No. 1* (1976; cat. no. 17) create a powerful feeling of expansion beyond the picture plane in a manner that recalls the paintings of Barnett Newman. The horizontal expansion of *Marsh Field No. 14* (1976; cat. no. 16) reminds one of the effects of Noland's horizontal band paintings, while *Floating Quadrangle No. 15* (1976; cat. no. 15) explores the relationship between interior and exterior shapes, a problem first articulated in the late 60s by Stella. Kinnee adapted the problem of the shaped canvas to printmaking by pouring liquid pulp into specially shaped deckles (cat. nos. 29–31). Although the paper, in shape and texture, carries most of the expression for Genn and Kinnee, both embellish it somewhat. Genn adds threads and fibers, embedding them into her surfaces. Kinnee uses his shaped paper as background for an etched or silkscreened composition.

Kinnee is not the only artist in the exhibition to use handmade paper as a means of redefining the traditional notion of a print. Sonnier and Royce also poured liquid pulp into molds of their own design. Sonnier's *Abaca-Code Series* (1976; cat. nos. 69 and 70) consists of prints on a monumental scale; Royce's *Frozen Motion Series* (1977; cat. nos. 53–55) are the first three-dimensional pyramidal shaped prints. In these examples, paper still functions as a background, since Sonnier's configurations were partially stamped, Royce's made by relief printing, and Kinnee's, as noted above, by etching or silk-screening. Although all three artists deal with problems of shape, color, and lines, Sonnier and Royce are not pure formalists. Sonnier's content comes partly from the use of hand-stamped letters. The Roman numerals which signify the artist's monogram, the date, and the series number, are as large as the geometric shapes of the design.[7] Royce's work always alludes to some subject or idea. Images of fish and the sea appear in the *Frozen Motion* pyramids and represent "the bringing into a new context the reality of the sea" and the reconciliation of counter currents, "one force opposing another in the flows of the lines."[8]

Clinton Hill's handmade paper "paintings" have been compared to Farnsworth's in that both incorporate graphic imagery within the paper. Hill stresses the significance of process in his work. As a painter working in the tradition of "Action Painting," he feels that the content of a work comes not just from formal relationships, but also from the fact that the work had to evolve; it has value as something which shaped and developed. Abstract forms are seen as something organic, which grow across the surface of a picture plane.

Even greater emphasis on paper art as a transformational process is expressed by Charles Christopher Hill, Al-Hilali, and O'Banion. Hill has stated that his foremost consideration is "the work and time spent on an individual work before it is finished."[9] Al-Hilali notes, "Most important of my objectives is the process of *transformation*. I work with the interaction of *physical structure and illusion*. Techniques of manipulation I invent as I work."[10] O'Banion makes her own paper and then recycles it into a second state. She views her work as a kind of metamorphosis, "creating one form, destroying it or altering it to give life to another form."[11] Content, then, for these artists is two-fold. On one level it comes from the material. Hill's *Je suis avec les anges* (1977; cat. no. 24), Al-Hilali's *Carpet Piece* (1977; cat. no. 5), and O'Banion's *Blue and Yellow Lining* (1977; cat. no.

45) are all abstract compositions where the paper conveys most of the expressive power, primarily through texture. But on a second level, one which appears more important to these artists, the paper provides the *means* for exploring elaborate conversions of a simple common material into highly organized, sophisticated, and powerful structures. According to Al-Hilali, this changes the traditional function of paper: "In my current work ...the effects often deny, conceal, obliterate the material. I subject the materials to various, in combination unorthodox treatment to evoke unexpected qualities, new experiences, more options."[12] Schwitters was probably the first artist to point out that the most common forms of paper—bits of letters, old postage stamps, wrapping paper, newspaper—could be considered valid components of a work of art, as exemplified by his *merz* collages of around 1920.

McCafferty also alters the appearance of a common material—graph paper. The grid of the paper enables control over the spacing and placement of solar burned configurations. Here, too, process is an important factor. Watching the images form allows the artist to observe matter in movement: "The sun moves during the day. That makes me move my body parallel to it, making me aware of the fact that nothing stays the same due to time putting its force in space."[13] On another level, McCafferty's art represents the creation of an object that alludes to nothing other than itself. The negative space of the solar burns allows the viewer to see the wall behind the work, and thus makes the autonomy of the object even more emphatic. Although the artist's primary focus is not upon visual relationships, his work is abstract and it is the material content—the tangibility of the paper as contrasted with negative space—which expresses the meaning on this second level.

While McCafferty is interested in objecthood, Alexander and Laubhan consider their art to be about formal relationships that suggest something beyond the physical appearance of the object. Both use an additive process, replicating predetermined shapes. Alexander considers the use of commercial paper rods to be a "psychological recycling of energy," sometimes representing a "mythic journey to the world of the dead."[14] Yet she places equal emphasis on the fact that the structures deal specifically with "the linear play of the rods against each other, and the planes they create."[15] Laubhan notes that the designs in her *New Lullabies Among Ancient Dances Series* (1977; cat. nos. 32 and 33) are reminiscent of architectural facades, but also states that "line, texture, shadows, surface treatment of the sheets, fiber embedded into the pulp, and the locking together of folded sheets all work together to form this dance in paper."[16] In the work of these two artists is the same kind of duality between content and form which presented itself in the collages and *papiers collés* of Braque and Picasso, only the paper now carries the entire expression.

Hilger, Smith, and Babcock also divide their attention between formal problems and the ideas thereby expressed. But each seeks to reveal an entirely different type of content. Hilger deals with associations drawn from the visual image; Smith works with written words and photographs; and Babcock employs a more traditional, less conceptual mode of subject. Yet for all, form and content are inseparable. Hilger restricts his formal vocabulary to white handmade paper in order to bring out the intrinsic properties of texture and shadow effects. He notes, "I know of no other medium that is as direct or as versatile as paper."[17] He also restricts his subject matter to paper products, such as packages (cat. nos. 20–22), and in this way forms an object which is simultaneously "of and about paper."[18] Smith achieves a similar integration of subject and form by mixing words and photos from magazines, books, and cigarette packages into the pulp. Much of the literary content is so finely ground that it is no longer recognizable as the original source. Bits and pieces of *Playboy Magazine* become formal elements, lending color, texture, and shape, but in a way that carries collage a step further: In a development parallel to others we have seen with handmade paper, they have become components of the physical make-up of the whole object, rather than pieces pasted on the surface. Like Hilger, Babcock views his art as an exploration of the expressive potential inherent in handmade paper: "My work is a reflection of my enjoyment, enchantment, and fascination with this material. I carefully form a sheet using a multi-colored pulp. The surface is treated with a great deal of respect. The power and strength of my work comes from an actual emotional response to this surface and underlying pulp."[19] But the subject matter is representational—three-dimensional topographical landscape. The significant aspect here, however, is that form and content are once again tightly bound together. Handmade paper (with color mixed directly into the pulp) can approximate the texture of the earth's surface more closely than bronze, stone, or other more conventional sculptor's materials.

Like Babcock, Neri applies handmade paper to a traditional subject. Neri's figure sculptures are made by casting pulp against molds of the human body, the same molds he uses when working with plaster. Making human figures from handmade paper enables new expressive qualities, which emerge from the texture, weight, and white color of the paper. The figures have been characterized as having "a delicate, almost ghostlike presence."[2]

Paris' work also falls within certain established traditions. The artist seeks to create personal, poetic imagery in a manner that recalls Cornell's boxes: through unexpected juxtaposition of objects. Paris imbeds objects into handmade paper while the pulp is still wet. The concern with personal imagery is not limited to the artist's work in paper, as he achieves similar results in his fiberglass sculptures. Handmade paper pieces, such as the *Soul Carta Series* (1975–76; cat. nos. 47 and 48) derive their meaning partly from the unusual juxtaposition subject matter and from poetic titles. But much of the expressive power comes from the textural effects of vacuum-formed edges and the rich saturation of colors which have been mixed into the pulp. So, although Paris is not a formalist, the nature of the material he employs nevertheless contributes strongly to the content of his work.

Nugent and Di Mare also aim at a kind of visual poetry and employ handmade paper and mixed media to that end. Both make small scale constructions associated with the sea. The small assemblages of Nugent's *Ancient Mariner Series* (1977; cat. nos. 41 and 42) depict the artist's conception of the remains of a shipwreck. Titles are based on actual historical records and some of the tiny "documents" of the ship are made by recycling antique letters. Although handmade paper is not the sole medium, its crisp and delicate surface lends a feeling of intimacy to the object. The same may be said of Di Mare's *Spirit Bundle No. 1* (1977; cat. no. 10) or *Triangular Oblation* (1977; cat. no. 11). To Di Mare, these images reflect his youthful experiences as a fisherman; he considers making paper to be like fishing in that one must first "catch" the pulp.

It is interesting to note that, like Di Mare, several artists in the exhibition explore autobiographical themes through the use of paper. The wax-coated paper sculptures of Schneider's *Here I Am Series* (1977; cat. nos. 62–66) each signify different psychological states of the artist's personality. Despite the abstract appearance of the sculptures, the artist's approach is conceptual. However, like some of the formalist artists, Schneider transforms paper into a new kind of object. She views the process of working with paper as a device for self-discovery: "Paper has always been a part of my work. It helps me to bring clarity into the chaos, and it lets me play."[21] Ruppersberg's *Personal Art Series* (1973; cat. nos. 58–61) is also conceptual in orientation. The artist's self-portrait was cut out from cardboard slabs, displayed alone or overlapping as a group, and from pieces of typing paper stacked compactly inside a cardboard carton. Ruppersberg always aims at an art that is personal, employs common material, and often includes the written word. He accomplished all of these goals expediently in the *Personal Art Series,* in an innovative manner: negative space carries the image while further meaning is conveyed by the titles, which form a major part of the composition in that they are handwritten on the cardboard surface. Also, the hanger in *Ready and Waiting* (cat. no. 60) acts as a visual pun for the mental state described by the title.

One of Royce's paper cast sculptures, *View Through My Window* (1977; cat. no. 57) also investigates the relationship between the artist and the world he lives in. By casting his studio window with handmade paper, Royce took a familiar object from his own everyday environment and placed it into a new context, forcing upon himself a reevaluation of that object. Although the artform exists as the impression rather than as actual object, Royce's gesture falls into a tradition begun by Rauschenberg in the 1950s, when the older artist made a combine painting from his own bed quilt.[22]

Rauschenberg was also one of the first artists to explore the potential of handmade paper. His influence on many of the younger artists has been pointed out by Richard Kubiak,[23] and Clinton Hill has noted that when he started to work with handmade paper, he "was not aware of others working in this medium with the exception of the Rauschenberg pieces that he had done in France."[24] From his combine paintings of the 1950s to his cardboard box collages of the early 70s, Rauschenberg has never hesitated to experiment with new materials. The *Bones* and *Unions* (1975; cat. nos. 49–52) are recent examples. The *Unions* were made from rag-mud, a mixture of pulp, mud, and spices. The rag-mud slabs were formed by hand and then joined into assemblage with string and bamboo. Like Royce, Kinnee, and Sonnier, Rauschenberg also redefined the traditional concept of printmaking, since the *Bones* and *Unions* were issued in multiples. He also forced one to evaluate previous conceptions about paper, since its basic ingredients were now modified to form a hard, coarsely textured three-dimensional object. Although not intended to be studies in form, Rauschenberg's pieces are always masterfully organized and elegant.

Perhaps it is with this thought in mind that one should view the exhibition. It is important, in understanding paper art, to be aware of the relation between content and form. To briefly review: content expresses itself in several ways—through process, by association, by representation, by expressive impact, or by concept. Because the form is paper, extended to most or all of the composition, form and content often merge at some point in their mutual interaction. But as to the matter of elegance and sophistication, the works in the exhibition speak for themselves.

D.S.R.

Notes

[1] For background on the growing number of paper mills in the United States see Marlene Schiller, "The American Community of Hand Papermakers," *American Artist,* LXI/421, August, 1977, pp. 39–44.

[2] Susan E. Meyer, "The Revolution in Paper," *American Artist* LXI/421, August, 1977, p. 33.

[3] Richard Kubiak, *The Handmade Paper Object,* The Santa Barbara Museum of Art, October 29–November 28, 1976, n.p.

[4] Braque made the first *papier collé* in 1912. It is entitled *Compotier et Verre* and is in the collection of Douglas Cooper, France. For further details regarding the invention of *papier collé* see John Golding, *Cubism, A History and Analysis 1907–1914,* p. 103 ff.

[5] This is in terms of Western art only. Eastern uses of paper, such as Japanese *origami* or Chinese paper cut-outs, is a larger issue which is beyond the scope of this essay.

[6] Golding, *op. cit.,* p. 106.

[7] There is also an important connection with Cubism here, as Braque and Picasso were the first artists to use letters as part of a composition. This was done for almost the same reason as the introduction of paper as formal element: to give references to the subject and at the same time clarify spatial relationships within the composition. See Golding, *op. cit.,* p. 92 ff or Robert Rosenblum, "Picasso and the Typography of Cubism," in Roland Penrose and John Golding (eds.), *Picasso in Retrospect,* New York, 1973, pp. 49–75.

[8] Richard Royce, response to a questionnaire, 1977.

[9] Charles Christopher Hill, response to a questionnaire, 1977.

[10] Neda Al-Hilali, statement, February, 1977.
[11] Nance O'Banion, response to a questionnaire, 1977.
[12] Al-Hilali, *op. cit.*
[13] Jay McCafferty, statement, 1977.
[14] Marsia Alexander, response to a questionnaire, 1977.
[15] *Ibid.*
[16] Karen Laubhan, response to a questionnaire, 1977.
[17] Charles Hilger, statement, 1977.
[18] *Ibid.*
[19] John Babcock, statement, 1977.
[20] Judith L. Dunham, "Manuel Neri: Woman," *Artweek,* VI/16, April 19, 1975, p. 16.
[21] Ursula Schneider, response to a questionnaire, 1977.
[22] *Bed* (1955; collection of Mr. and Mrs. Leo Castelli, New York), reproduced in Andrew Forge, *Rauschenberg,* New York, 1969, p. 180.
[23] Kubiak, *op. cit.*
[24] Clinton Hill, response to a questionnaire, 1977.

CATALOGUE

3 Marsia Alexander, *Four Voices,* 1977

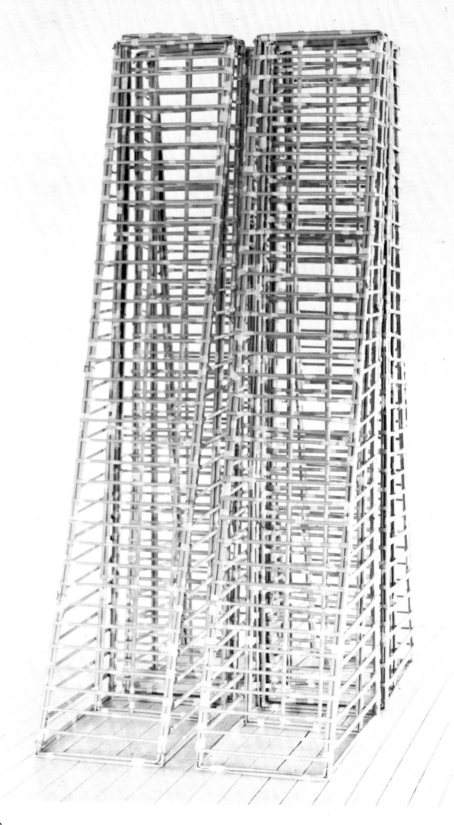

Marsia Alexander
b. 1939

1 *Vehicle No. 1,* 1977
Paper, tape and rhoplex
8 x 2½ x 1 ft.
Lent by the Vanguard Gallery, Los Angeles

2 *Vehicle No. 2,* 1977
Paper, tape and rhoplex
8 x 2½ ft. x 10 in.
Lent by Vanguard Gallery, Los Angeles

3 *Four Voices,* 1977
Paper, tape and rhoplex
8 x 4 x 4 ft.
Lent by Vanguard Gallery, Los Angeles

Marsia Alexander's sculptures use rolled paper rods as a means of drawing in and delineating three-dimensional space. Each object, whether freestanding or attached to the wall, is built of individual rods of wrapping paper which intersect with open space and at the same time entrap it. The cage-like structure of *Four Voices* (1977; cat. no. 3) encloses an area of space which would otherwise be negative—thus making it seem visible, tangible, and hence, positive. Viewed from different angles, Alexander's works present a variety of patterns of lines and planes, formed by the overlapping and intersection of rods against one another.

Alexander began working with paper around 1971. At that time she shifted from making paintings which emphasized edges and contours, to making relief paintings on paper with edges formed from the folding of paper. Gradually she turned to building structures from scroll-shaped components and, through reduction of her format to its most skeletal framework, developed the present syntax.

Each sculpture is constructed of paper pieces which are cut to specific lengths, rolled, taped, and tied together. Many of the sculptures are then painted and, once complete, all are coated with rhoplex.

Alexander's titles are suggested by the finished image. The artist views *Four Voices* as a visual metaphor for a choral reading in that the structure contains "the same type of amassing intersecting with pause."[1] The *Vehicles* (1977; cat. nos. 1 and 2) are so named due to their resemblance to sleds.

[1]Marsia Alexander, response to a questionnaire, 1977.

Bibliography
Suzanne Muchnic, "Marsia Alexander's Sculptural Wrappings," *Artweek,* VIII/24, July 2, 1977, p. 6.

Neda Al-Hilali
b. 1938

4 *Althee,* 1977
Paper, knotted and woven
100 x 92 in.
Lent by Vanguard Gallery, Los Angeles

5 *Carpet Piece,* 1977
Paper, knotted and woven
52 x 44 in.
Lent by David and Cloyce Flaten, La Verne, California

A seemingly endless range of procedures is employed by Neda Al-Hilali as she transforms interwoven pieces of ordinary paper into vigorous large scale constructions. Al-Hilali plaits together continuous lengths of paper which she has treated in a variety of ways. Her methods include crumpling, folding, hammering, pressing, soaking, dying, burnishing, scorching, and treating the paper with chemicals or glue. Sometimes a work is painted for coloristic effects, while other examples express themselves primarily through texture. Both characteristics are evident in *Carpet Piece* (1977; cat. no. 5), depending upon the location of the viewer. Seen up close, the work exhibits a coloristically rich pattern of intricately interwoven lines. From a distance it is more textural, with a strong interplay of light and shadow created out of the repeated folds.

Al-Hilali was originally a fiber artist, but found that working with paper offered her greater flexibility and a broader spectrum of effects:

As I became more conscious of the potential of the fiber medium, its limitations also became more apparent. The most pernicious problem of fiber is its almost insurmountable buoyancy with regard to its recognizable physical character and established associations. Therefore, I moved from the rather *specific* fiber to a more *neutral* material, which is more susceptible to transformations, even mutations; whose physical and plastic qualities in the form of paper pulp are contrasted, balanced by its long-standing association with non-material endeavors, as the traditional vehicle for intellectual and illusionistic communication.[1]

In addition to wall pieces, the artist makes enormous freestanding sculptures through the same process.[2]

[1]Neda Al-Hilali, quoted in Bernard Kester, "The Paper Constructions of Neda-Al Hilali," *Craft Horizons,* XXVI/1, February, 1976, p. 31.
[2]See *ibid.* for reproductions of these works.

5 Neda Al-Hilali, *Carpet Piece*, 1977

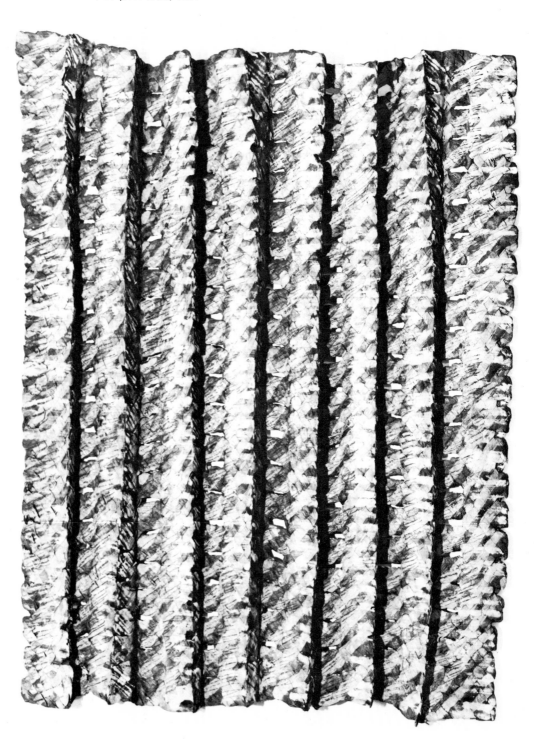

Bibliography
Bernard Kester, "The Paper Constructions of Neda Al-Hilali," *Craft Horizons,* XXXVI/1, February, 1976, pp. 30–33 ff.

Robert McDonald, "Genn and Al-Hilali—Works in Paper," *Artweek,* VIII/8, February 19, 1977, p. 3. Suzanne Muchnic, "Neda Al-Hilali and Paul Soldner," *Artweek,* VII/35, October 16, 1976, p. 6.

John Babcock
b. 1941

6 *Trace Through a Late Arizona Afternoon,* 1976
Handmade paper
32 x 32 in.
Lent by the Artist

7 *Malibu Winter Trace,* 1977
Handmade paper
21 x 21 in.
Lent by the Artist

8 *Tehachapi Winter Morning Fissure,* 1977
Handmade paper
35 x 35 in.
Lent by the Artist

9 *Whitney Meadow Winter Sky Trace,* 1977
Handmade paper
31 x 31 in.
Lent by Harrison Gill, Santa Maria, California

John Babcock uses wet pulp of 100% cotton fiber to form abstract topographical landscapes. Works like *Tehachapi Winter Morning Fissure* (1977; cat. no. 8) have been split into two sections, either by pulling apart slightly the freshly poured pulp, or by separating it with part of a curved mat board or a palette knife. In the various *Traces* (cat. nos. 6, 7, and 9) patterns are formed from tooling the pulp with a broad stylus, or by the impression made when excess wet pulp is swiftly flung against the surface. In this manner, Babcock simulates the effects of earthquakes, meteors, or other phenomena that alter the structure of topographical surfaces. Limitation of color to earth tones is thus deliberate. Many different earth pigments are beaten into the pulp, but not to the degree that they blend into a single hue. Rather, the artist leaves the pulp multi-colored as a way of further evoking the appearance of the earth's or, in some instances, the moon's surface.

The artist also views his work as an exploration of the intrinsic qualities of handmade paper: "The paper pulp is essentially the same material used hundreds of years ago for fine paper. I am actually working in the paper and not just on the surface. Various kinds of pulp give me the texture and consistency that I require... In concept I feel I am using this new and ancient material in a traditional manner. The paper records the response, action, and becomes a visual idea."[1]

Babcock began working in handmade paper in his studio in 1974, using it for deeply embossed prints. He learned to manipulate wet pulp the following year at Garner Tullis' International Institute for Experimental Printmaking.

[1] John Babcock, statement, 1977.

Bibliography

Judith Durham, "New Forms in Paper," *Craft Horizons,* XXXVI/2, April, 1976, pp. 38–43 ff.
Richard Kubiak, *The Handmade Paper Object,* The Santa Barbara Museum of Art, October 29–November 28, 1976.
Suzi Thomasen, "John Babcock's Earth Surfaces," *Artweek,* VIII/18, April 30, 1977, p. 4.

Dominic L. Di Mare
b. 1932

10 *Spirit Bundle No. 1,* 1977
Handmade paper, wood, raffia, feathers and linen thread
15 x 18 x 9 in.
Lent by the Artist

11 *Triangular Oblation,* 1977
Handmade paper, wood, raffia, feather and bone
10 x 10 x 11 in.
Lent by the Artist

The small, delicate, intricate constructions of Dominic L. Di Mare are limited to only a few materials. Small pieces of hand formed paper are compacted within frameworks of hawthorn wood, tied together and embellished with string, feathers, bones, felt, or fibers. Each object displays a subtle elegance, which may be seen in the even rhythm of the wooden contours of *Spirit Bundle No. 1* (1977; cat. no. 10) or in the flowing movement of the fibers drifting slowly off the wooden frame of *Triangular Oblation* (1977; cat. no. 11).

Di Mare's art is highly personal in two respects: it reflects both his present and his past. The materials from which he constructs are gathered from his home environment (his own trees, the surrounding beaches), often with the help of his wife and children. The family has also assisted in pressing out the paper. But it is the artist's deep feelings about his childhood which govern both the process and content of his work: "Much of my youth was spent with my father, a commercial fisherman, fishing off the coasts of California and Mexico. The whole process of making paper, for me, mirrors that important part of my life."[1] The artist sees an analogy between "catching the pulp" and fishing from the sea. The materials—bones, wood, feathers—recall Di Mare's early years in that these are the elements from which the fisherman builds his tools.

Prior to using handmade paper (which he began doing in 1970), Di Mare was making large woven sculptures.

13

[1]Dominic L. Di Mare, statement, 1977.

Bibliography
Margery Anneberg, "Dominic Di Mare," *Craft Horizons,* XXXVI/1, February, 1976, p. 61.
Mary Fuller, "Paper, Wood, and String of Dominic Di Mare," *Craft Horizons,* XXXVII/3, June, 1977, pp. 52–55.
Richard Kubiak, *The Handmade Paper Object,* The Santa Barbara Museum of Art, October 29–November 28, 1976.

Don Farnsworth
b. 1951

12   *Untitled,* 1977
Handmade paper
17 x 27½ in.
Lent by ADI Gallery, San Francisco

13   *Untitled,* 1977
Handmade paper
26½ x 22 in.
Lent by ADI Gallery, San Francisco

14   *JP-Four Squares No. 1,* 1977
Handmade paper
17 x 27½ in.
Lent by ADI Gallery, San Francisco

Don Farnsworth became intrigued with the properties of paper while studying paper conservation at an Oakland paper laboratory. He bought his first piece of papermaking equipment in 1973 and soon thereafter began operating his own paper mill, presently located in San Francisco. Several artists have collaborated with Farnsworth in making handmade paper pieces, among them Nancy Genn and Harold Paris, both of whom are represented in the current exhibition.

Farnsworth has devised a system for painting and drawing directly on the surface of a freshly couched sheet of paper with liquid pulp. As a result, the compositional configurations are imbedded *within* rather than on top of the surface and thus become part of the paper itself. The artist notes that, "By combining traditional papermaking methods with certain modern techniques and chemicals, I have developed and modified many processes which allow me to work directly with paper in a way never before possible. I consider 'paper pulp drawing' to be one of the more important developments."[1]

The artist attains his colors by using the Hollander beater to finely grind cotton pulp which has been dyed with fiber reactive phocion dyes. Unlike pigments, this substance will tend not to bleed when applied to wet pulp, a factor which enables Farnsworth to maintain a distinct separation between figure and ground. The mode of application may vary. In *Untitled* (1977; cat. no. 12), the liquid pulp was applied with a water jet to create a relief-like surface, even eating away parts of the couched sheet. A watercolor-like effect was attained in *JP-Four Squares No. 1* (1977; cat. no. 14) and *Untitled* (1977; cat. no. 13) by administering the colored pulp through a tube.

[1]Don Farnsworth, statement, 1977.

Bibliography
Marlene Schiller, "The American Community of Hand Papermakers," *American Artist,* XLI/421, August, 1977, p. 41.

Nancy Genn

15   *Floating Quadrangle No. 15,* 1976
Embossed handmade paper, mohair and thread
35 x 43 in.
Lent by Susan Caldwell Gallery, New York City

16   *Marsh Field No. 14,* 1976
Handmade paper (in collaboration with Don Farnsworth)
34 x 62 in.
Lent by Susan Caldwell Gallery, New York City

17   *Uxmall No. 1,* 1976
Embossed handmade paper (in collaboration with Don Farnsworth)
42 x 38 in.
Lent by Susan Caldwell Gallery, New York City

18   *Arapaho No. 1,* 1977
Embossed handmade paper, laminated hand-colored mulberry paper and wool
22½ x 26 in.
Lent by Susan Caldwell Gallery, New York City

19   *Rain Bar Drawing,* 1977
Embossed handmade paper, mohair and pencil (in collaboration with Don Farnsworth)
32 x 37 in.
Lent by Susan Caldwell Gallery, New York City

Through careful layering and manipulation of strips of handmade paper, Nancy Genn creates wall pieces that combine elements of painting and relief. By varying the size, position, texture, and color of the different bands of fresh pulp, the artist

13 Don Farnsworth, *Untitled,* 1977

18 Nancy Genn, *Arapaho No. 1,* 1977

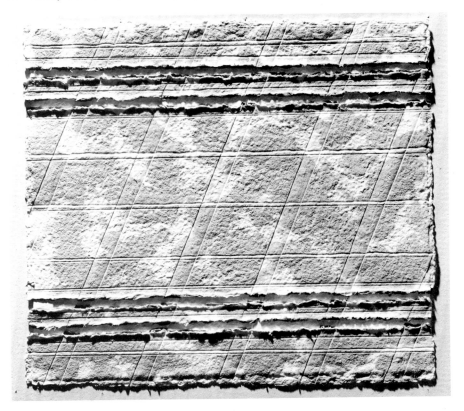

conveys a variety of temperaments, ranging from the lyrically cool to the brutally aggressive.

Originally a painter and sculptor, Genn has been working exclusively with handmade paper since 1975, when she purchased her own Hollander beater for shredding rags into pulp. She has also worked in the paper workshops of Garner Tullis, John Koller, and Don Farnsworth.

Genn views her current work as an outgrowth of her earlier art. She first experimented with paper as medium in the early 1960s by making large mural size paintings on imported oversized rag paper. The recent handmade paper pieces continue formal concerns which may be observed in the artist's paintings of the early 1970s. For example, the free-floating linear rhythms in the ground of *Arapaho No. 1* (1977; cat. no. 18), as well as the horizontal bands at top and bottom, restate somewhat the compositional structure of a 1974 acrylic painting, *Saratoga*.[1] The paper work, however, allows for the added dimensions of texture and relief.

Genn has described her basic working procedure:

First the sheet is formed and couched onto a felt. The image is developed using pre-dyed pulp that has been separately beaten in the Hollander beater. Threads and tissues are placed on top of the first sheet of pulp. Often two or even three additional layers of paper are couched on top of the first. Layers beneath are revealed according to a predetermined plan.[2]

Depending on the desired result, the artist adds other materials to the layered strips of paper. Subtle accents are achieved by stringing pieces of thread, mohair, silk, wool, alpaca, or rice paper between layers of pulp, either parallel to the bands, or crossing them diagonally. Genn also varies the composition of the pulp itself. In *Marsh Field No. 14* (1976; cat. no. 16) the gray pulp was finely ground and applied as pigment on top of the blue bars, while in *Uxmall No. 1* (1976; cat. no. 17) the pulp was deliberately left coarse so that the rag fibers could activate the surface texturally.

[1] Reproduced in *Artweek,* V/30, September 14, 1974, p. 4.
[2] Nancy Genn, response to a questionnaire, 1977.

Bibliography

Sandy Ballatore, *Nancy Genn, John Okulick, Jack Scott, Leo Valledor,* Los Angeles Institute of Contemporary Art, September 21–October 14, 1976.
David Bourdon, "Pulp Artists Paper MOMA," *The Village Voice,* August 23, 1976.
Richard Kubiak, *The Handmade Paper Object,* The Santa Barbara Museum of Art, October 29–November 28, 1976.
Robert McDonald, "Genn and Al-Hilali—Works in Paper," *Artweek,* VIII/8, Februray 19, 1977, p. 8.

Charles Hilger
b. 1938

20 *SEGMENTS: PACKAGE No. 22,* 1977
Vacuum-formed paper
30 x 16 x 5 in.
Lent by Smith Andersen Gallery, Palo Alto

21 *SEGMENTS: PACKAGE No. 24,* 1977
Vacuum-formed paper
30 x 16 x 2 in.
Lent by Smith Andersen Gallery, Palo Alto

22 *SEGMENTS: PACKAGE No. 32,* 1977
Vacuum-formed paper
64 x 54 x 6 in. (framed)
Lent by Smith Andersen Gallery, Palo Alto

Charles Hilger writes, "My work is completely of and about paper. I make my own material from cotton linters and have been working with paper exclusively since 1974. My work is all white: I am interested in the shadows and variations thereof that the paper itself created. Therefore, I use no other color or material. I know of no other medium that is as direct or as versatile as paper. I believe contemporary society depends overwhelmingly upon paper as a carrier of image and a supporting element for statement. I am dealing with the fact that paper itself is now becoming primary image and statement in society's art."[1]

In other words, Hilger's paper reliefs and sculptures are intended to be expressive on both a formal and conceptual level. This duality may be seen in *SEGMENTS: PACKAGE No. 22* (1977; cat. no. 20): separate sheets of handmade paper have been stacked and tightly compacted to form a box-like or package-shaped structure. The image is delicate and fragile. Deckled edges ripple across the surface, animating and enlivening it. By folding over and crumpling paper in the front plane, Hilger has allowed for a dramatic play of light and shadow. Yet the artist has noted that here he is also "dealing with (his) ideas of how contemporary society 'packages' itself," but leaves any subjective interpretation of the individual paper segments up to the viewer.[2]

Hilger continues to explore the numerous possibilities of a basic vocabulary that is limited to white sheets of handmade paper, its edges and flat planes. His recent work has become more sculptural than earlier endeavors such as *Box No. 21* (1975),[3] where the work was basically flat,

with a minimum of relief achieved by scoring and folding forward portions of the paper.

[1] Charles Hilger, statement, 1977.
[2] Charles Hilger, letter to David S. Rubin, September 10, 1977.
[3] Reproduced in Judith Von Euer, "Charles Hilger Hand-Formed Paper," *Artweek,* VII/9, February 28, 1976, p. 7.

Bibliography

Judith Von Euer, "Charles Hilger Hand-Formed Paper," *Artweek,* VII/9, February 28, 1976, p. 7.
Richard Kubiak, *The Handmade Paper Object,* The Santa Barbara Museum of Art, October 29–November 28, 1976.
Martha Spelman, "Jerry Byrd and Charles Hilger," *Artweek,* VIII/14, April 2, 1977, p. 8.

Charles Christopher Hill
b. 1948

23   *Black, Orange, Beige,* 1972
Stitched paper backed with cloth
69 x 93 in.
Lent by the Artist

24   *Je suis avec les anges,* 1977
Stitched paper backed with cloth
69 x 56½ in.
Lent by Cirrus Gallery, Los Angeles

The initial attraction to paper, for Charles Christopher Hill, was that it was free and readily available. In 1971 he abandoned the use of paints, which he found messy and bothersome, in favor of the process that he uses today. Pieces of paper of all types—including rag, newsprint, construction paper, and crepe paper—are sewn together on a cloth backing and sometimes in conjunction with pieces of fabric. In early pieces, such as *Black, Orange, Beige* (1972; cat. no. 23) the stitching served as a kind of drawing in that it was prominent and very calligraphic. The horizontal bands of color, a configuration which derives from earlier minimal paintings, were made from crepe paper and when wet, bled into other areas of the composition. More recent works, such as *Je suis avec les anges* (1977; cat. no. 24), are less graphic, with greater emphasis on the raw surface effects of the paper itself.

Although Hill's technique provides the means for scores of large scale formalist compositions, his primary interest lies in the process itself: "My main concern is not the end product but the work and time spent on an individual work before it is finished. I sometimes think that compromising the integrity of my original idea for each individual piece is the main goal and the end product of all my work."[1] A work is begun with no backing and with both sides of the composition in mind. The side that pleases the artist first is preserved and developed towards its final state. The last stage of the process involves putting the work through a kind of durability test, first mutilating it and then repairing it: "I construct my works to be strong and then subject them to abuses that will destroy the finished product of my work. The most important part of what I do is the restoration of a piece. I may restore and destroy something three or four times."[2]

[1] Charles Christopher Hill, response to a questionnaire, 1977.
[2] *Ibid.*

Bibliography

Allen Ellenzweig, "4 California Artists," *Arts Magazine,* L/5, January, 1976, pp. 23–24.
Peter Frank, "Works on Paper," *Art News,* LXXV/1, January, 1976, p. 127.
Melinda Wortz, "The 'Cool School'," *Art News,* LXV/6, Summer, 1976, pp. 142–146.

23   Charles Christopher Hill, *Black, Orange, Beige,* 1972

Clinton Hill
b. 1922

25   *No. 52,* 1975
     Handmade paper, 1/6
     22½ x 17½ in.
     Lent by William Sawyer Gallery,
     San Francisco

26   *No. 70,* 1975
     Handmade paper, 2/5
     22½ x 17½ in.
     Lent by William Sawyer Gallery,
     San Francisco

27   *No. 77,* 1975
     Handmade paper, 1/5
     22½ x 17½ in.
     Lent by William Sawyer Gallery,
     San Francisco

28   *Woodstock Village Road,* 1976
     Handmade paper
     22¾ x 18 in.
     Lent by William Sawyer Gallery,
     San Francisco

Clinton Hill's artistic roots lie somewhere in the realm of the first generation of the New York School. His attitude towards his abstract paintings has always emphasized the notion of art as pro-

cess. In 1974 Hill commented, "I guess I was heavily influenced by the 50's...I still see painting as a way of getting from one side of the canvas to the other."[1] At the time, he was making relief-paintings by manipulating fiberglass on canvas to yield varying patterns of color and richly textured surfaces.[2]

Hill turned to working with handmade paper almost as an afterthought. In 1973–74, while doing a group of drawings by tearing and cutting unmarked sheets of paper, he considered the possible flexibility of working in a similar fashion with wet pulp. So he visited the paper mill of John Koller, only to be fascinated by another aspect of the paper making process: "I became intrigued by the possibilities of using watermark as drawing."[3]

Hill has experimented with this idea over the past few years and developed a full vocabulary of techniques. The point of departure for a composition is usually the watermark, which the artist designs by arranging wires on the mold. The pulp is then poured over this and the composition is underway. Formal changes occur through the addition of dyes and color pigments, sometimes spooned into a template, or by the application of

18

layers of viled pulp to small areas of pulp in conjunction with large amounts of water. The latter procedure allows color areas to bleed into the white background. Although the specific methods of applying pulp may vary slightly, the result is always a sheet of richly textured handmade paper which like a painting, contains a division between figure and ground. In *No. 52* (1975; cat. no. 25) for example, the colored pigments simulate the effect of broad and rapidly applied brushstrokes, and stand in sharp contrast to the white background.

The artist considers his paper pieces to be supplemental to his activity as a painter and treats them as a kind of printmaking—produced both as single sheets and in multiples.

[1] Clinton Hill, quoted in Gerrit Henry, "The Permitting Medium, A Note on the Art of Clinton Hill," *Art International,* XVIII/6, Summer, 1974, p. 58.
[2] Descriptions of Hill's fiberglass paintings may be found *ibid* and also in Michael Andre, "Clinton Hill," *Art News,* LXXII/9, November, 1973, p. 107.
[3] Clinton Hill, response to a questionnaire, 1977.

Bibliography
Gordon Brown, "Clinton Hill," *Arts Magazine,* L/1, September, 1975, p. 23.
Richard Kubiak, *The Handmade Paper Object,* The Santa Barbara Museum of Art, October 29–November 28, 1976.

25 Clinton Hill, *No. 52,* 1975

Sandy Kinnee
b. 1947

29 *Light Showers and Downpour/Ladies Silver Fan,* 1976
Etching on handmade paper, 6/7
20 x 21 in.
Lent by ADI Gallery, San Francisco

30 *Ogallala/On Thin Ice,* 1976
Screen print on handmade paper, 17/17
23 x 22 in.
Lent by ADI Gallery, San Francisco

31 *Call You/Coral Necklace,* 1977
Screen print on handmade paper, 5/15
20½ x 20½ in.
Lent by ADI Gallery, San Francisco

In Sandy Kinnee's work, paper retains its traditional role as background surface; handmade paper is Kinnee's answer to the problem of the shaped print.

During 1974–75 Kinnee was painting in a way that allowed the paint itself to determine the shape of a painting. The large scale shaped paintings were very fragile and difficult to transport. So, in 1975 the artist learned papermaking at Wayne State University in Detroit and began etching and screenprinting on handshaped paper. The artist sees the advantages of this as "greater control over the shape, more durability, and easier display" of his art.[1]

Kinnee's shaped prints are issued in multiples: "From each shaped deckle I cast I make from 10 to 150 sheets."[2] The artist's vocabulary of shapes includes spirals, such as *Call You/Coral Necklace* (1977; cat. no. 31) and fans (cat. no. 29). His procedure offers endless possibilities.

[1] Sandy Kinnee, response to a questionnaire, 1977.
[2] *Ibid.*

Karen Laubhan
b. 1943

32 *New Lullabies Among Ancient Dances Series No. 3,* 1977
Cotton, linen, sisal and denim
26 x 26 in. (mounted)
Lent by the Artist

33 *New Lullabies Among Ancient Dances Series No. 8,* 1977
Cotton, linen, sisal and colored roving
30 x 36 in. (mounted)
Lent by the Artist

32   Karen Laubhan, *New Lullabies Among Ancient Dances Series No. 3,* 1977

34   *Pockets Series,* 1977
     Cotton, linen and graphite
     15 x 18 in. (12 units)
     Lent by the Artist

35   *Pockets Series No. 3,* 1977
     Cotton, sisal and denim
     48 x 39 in. (100 units)
     Lent by the Artist

Karen Laubhan enjoys constructing with hand-made paper because it is softer and more flexible than traditional sculpting materials, such as wood, metal, or stone.[1] Since 1974, when Laubhan became aware of the paper experiments at the International Institute for Experimental Print-making, the artist has made paper sculptures from her own pulp.

Laubhan is interested in building forms which are rich in texture. For this reason she mixes sisal fibers into the pulp. This particular fiber will not break down in the Hollander beater and thus becomes part of the paper itself, while also strengthening it.

The *Pockets Series* (1977; cat. nos. 34 and 35) is based on a modular system. A chosen shape and pattern is repeated in equal units with drama-tic results. In the larger example (1977; cat. no. 35) bold patterns emerge from the deep shad-ows of the pockets, made by gently folding the paper while still damp, as well as from the subtle variance of color. Laubhan never works with pigments. Color is determined from the material (usually clothing—denim for blue) which is shredded into the pulp. Less obvious is the mod-ular structure which underlies the *New Lullabies Among Ancient Dances Series* (1977; cat. nos. 32 and 33). Paper strips of equal length were allowed to dry and then folded along the watermark (the weakest point in the paper), curled by hand, and stuck together with a silicone based glue. When the piece is finished, one is no longer aware that each strip is the same size. Instead we find a relief sculpture with rhythmic interaction between light and shadow and sensi-tive contrast between the hand-folded hard edges and the softer edges made by the deckle.

The artist views her attraction to modules as an extension of an interest in the structure of the environment. She notes that modern archi-tecture and nature itself are often formed in modular units.[2]

[1]Karen Laubhan, phone conversation with David S. Rubin, October 2, 1977.
[2]*Ibid.*

Bibliography

Richard Kubiak, *The Handmade Paper Object,* The Santa Barbara Museum of Art, October 29–November 28, 1976.

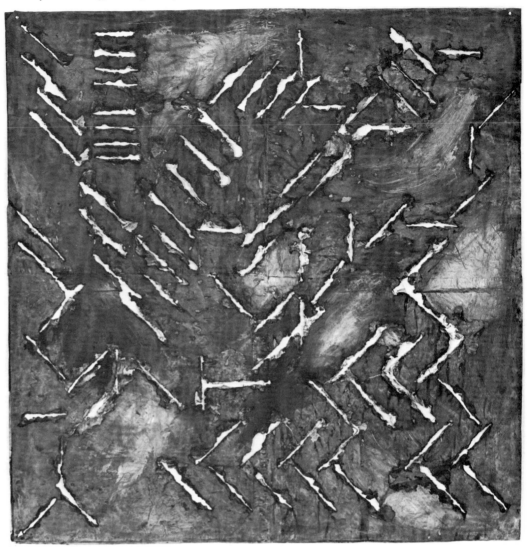

Jay McCafferty
b. 1948

36 *Untitled,* 1974
Solar burns on paper
3 x 3 ft.
Lent by Cirrus Gallery, Los Angeles

37 *Untitled,* 1977
Solar burns on paper
3 x 3 ft.
Lent by Cirrus Gallery, Los Angeles

38 *Participation,* 1977
Solar burns on rusted and inked paper
6 x 6 ft.
Lent by Cirrus Gallery, Los Angeles

Solar burning is a process which Jay McCafferty
developed in 1972 and has continued to use with
varied results. Compositions emerge on paper
(he also employs canvas, wood, and plastic) at a
slow pace as a consequence of the sun's heat,
which penetrates through a hand held magnifying
glass to ignite small areas of the paper. The
earlier solar burned images consist of patterns of
holes, evenly spaced because they have been
plotted along the grid of rag vellum graph paper.
When the paper is allowed to char, as in *Untitled*
(1974; cat. no. 36), a great amount of interior
movement and vitality results. Yet tight and careful control of the burning can also turn a sheet
of graph paper into an object of extreme fragility,
as exemplified by *Untitled* (1977; cat. no. 37). In
McCafferty's most recent work, such as *Participation* (1977; cat. no. 38), tiny holes have been

replaced by linear configurations which have burned through more than one layer of paper. By moving the magnifying glass horizontally, vertically, or diagonally, the artist can now "draw" with solar energy.

McCafferty's is an art of objecthood: "I like the idea of a real object that is made up, and how it was made with no illusion or allusion but itself and no more."[1] It is an art of constancy as well as uniqueness: "My work is about the repeated image of similar things that are slightly different due to the fact that all matter is in a state of movement...Every hole is made the same way yet all holes are very different."[2] The artist is able to exercise control (in the movement and positioning of the magnifying glass, for example), while simultaneously exploiting the effects of chance and natural phenomena.

[1]Jay McCafferty, statement, 1977.
[2]*Ibid.*

Bibliography
Sandy Ballatore, "Jay McCafferty at Cirrus," *Art in America,* LXIV/2, March–April, 1976, pp. 114–115.
Sandy Ballatore, "Jay McCafferty Solar Burns," *Artweek,* VI/38, November 8, 1975, pp. 1, 16.
Suzanne Muchnic, "Jay McCafferty: *Truth,*" *Artweek,* VIII/11, March 12, 1977, p. 6.
Elizabeth Perlmutter, "Hotbed of Advanced Art," *Art News,* LXXV/1, January, 1976, pp. 44–46.

Manuel Neri
b. 1930

39 *Back,* 1974
Cast handmade paper
43½ x 24 in.
Lent by Braunstein/Quay Gallery, San Francisco

40 *Torso,* 1974
Cast handmade paper
5 x 13 x 14 in.
Lent by Braunstein/Quay Gallery, San Francisco

Manuel Neri's concern with the human figure has remained constant throughout a career that dates back to the early 1950s. A 1976 retrospective exhibition at the Oakland Museum demonstrated the artist's ability to ponder the human form in several media, ranging from assemblage, to plaster cast figures, and, more recently, to paper cast images.[1]

Neri uses handmade paper in the same manner that he employs plaster. The wet pulp is cast on the same molds used for plaster pieces to form fragments of human anatomy. Working in both media simultaneously allows the artist to ponder questions about surface and weight of the images he creates. While a plaster fragment must be mounted on a metal rod for support, a paper version can hang freely from a nail tacked on the wall.

Neri's white rugged surfaces possess an expressive potential which has caused his style to be compared to that of Giacometti and George Segal.[2]

[1]See Judith L. Dunham, "Manuel Neri: Life with the Figure," *Artweek,* VII/39, November 13, 1976, pp. 1, 7.
[2]Such a comparison was made in Peter Frank, "Manuel Neri," *Art News,* LXXV/5, May, 1976, p. 128.

Bibliography
Thomas Albright, "Slouching Mortality and Inky Galaxies," *Art News,* LXXVI/1, January, 1977, pp. 90–92.
Judith L. Dunham, "Manuel Neri: Life with the Figure," *Artweek,* VII/39, November 13, 1976, pp. 1, 7.
Peter Frank, "Manuel Neri," *Art News,* LXXVI/1, January, 1977, p. 128.
Richard Kubiak, *The Handmade Paper Object,* The Santa Barbara Museum of Art, October 29–November 28, 1976.

Bob Nugent
b. 1947

41 *Nassau 1826* (from *Ancient Mariner Series*), 1977
Handmade paper and mixed media
22 x 18½ x 3 in.
Lent by Grapestake Gallery, San Francisco

42 *Raffaele 1896* (from *Ancient Mariner Series*), 1977
Handmade paper and mixed media
22½ x 13⅓ x 3 in.
Lent by Grapestake Gallery, San Francisco

43 *Ocean Notes,* 1977
Handmade paper
9½ x 15¼ in.
Lent by Grapestake Gallery, San Francisco

44 *Scribe's Notes,* 1977
Handmade paper
12 x 13 in.
Lent by Grapestake Gallery, San Francisco

Nostalgia, poetry, and fantasy are expressed by Bob Nugent in his handmade paper constructions. The artist has made envelopes which he fills with what he imagines would be the effects, tools, documents, and other memorabilia left from a shipwreck: "these might include epistles of authority, tokens, love letters, and all of those found and functional objects that contribute to the minutiae of our lives."[1] Collectively these works make up the *Ancient Mariner Series.* Nugent forms the ship's paraphernalia from handmade paper, twine, and twigs. Sometimes an added sense of history is wrought from the recycling of 17th and 18th century letters into new sheets of paper. Titles like *Raffaele 1896* (1977; cat. no. 42) and *Nassau 1826* (1977; cat. no. 41) refer to vessels which have sunk off Sable Island in the

North Atlantic, and are taken from actual records. The artist also draws inspiration from his own experiences of the sea and from correspondence with other sea adventurers.

Nugent learned to make a kind of Mulberry paper in 1971, while studying and teaching in the Samoan Islands. He has worked with 100% rag paper since 1973.

[1] Bob Nugent, statement, 1977.

Bibliography
Richard Kubiak, *The Handmade Paper Object,* The Santa Barbara Museum of Art, October 29–November 28, 1976.
Robert McDonald, "Visual Poetry by Shaw and Nugent," *Artweek,* VIII/26, July 30, 1977, p. 6.

Nance O'Banion
b. 1949

45   *Blue and Yellow Lining* (from *Folded Quilted Flap Series*), 1977
Handmade paper, dye, pigment and crayon
12 x 15 in.
Lent by The Allrich Gallery, San Francisco

46   *Quilted Pocket Series,* 1977
Handmade paper, dye, pigment and stitching
6 x 6 ft. (16 units)
Lent by The Allrich Gallery, San Francisco

"Reconstruction and manipulation" are terms which Nance O'Banion feels best describe her

approach to art.[1] Formerly a textile artist, O'Banion moved with ease to working with handmade paper, using it in a manner similar to her textile procedures. She begins by constructing a piece of paper from her own blended pulp (poured onto a screen) and then recycling it, "cutting it up and remaking it into another by coating it in more pulp."[2] The next step involves building new forms from the recycled paper. In the *Quilted Pocket Series* (1977; cat. no. 46), flaps and pockets were made by inserting handiwipes between layers of raw pulp. Once the layered surfaces are finished, the artist works them further with the addition of dyes, inks, crayon, and hand or machine stitching. Of this she writes, "I feel that this final metamorphosis gives life, energy, and emotion to the works. When the personality is complete, I no longer feel a part of my works as each has its own identity and character."[3]

Scale and texture are both important for O'Banion. The *Quilted Pocket Series* is one of the artist's largest works, constructed from modular units. This method satisfied her goal that "every paper have a strong graphic power at a distance as well as a seductive delicacy up close."[4] The viewer may choose to focus on each piece individually, or note the unity of the composition as a whole, as several patterns of line, shape, and color are born from selective placement of each module on the wall. The quilt-like texture of this series, as well as that of *Blue and Yellow Lining* (1977; cat. no. 45), was formed by casting the wet pulp against plastic nursery bedding and provides a further link between the artist's present work and her earlier fabric pieces.

[1]Nance O'Banion, response to a questionnaire, 1977.
[2]*Ibid.*
[3]*Ibid.*
[4]*Ibid.*

Harold Paris
b. 1925

47 *Kind Bees Consoling a Devastated Citadel* (from *Soul Carta Series*), 1976
Pressed paper imbeds
31 x 26 x 4½ in. (framed)
Lent by Smith Andersen Gallery, Palo Alto

48 *Wayfarer: The Dusk Hours Which Stands Before* (from *Soul Carta Series*), 1976
Pressed paper imbeds
42 x 30½ x 3½ in. (framed)
Lent by Smith Andersen Gallery, Palo Alto

In 1972 Peter Selz described the *oeuvre* of Harold Paris: "Technology, politics, life, death, sex, poetry, love, and art: all are converted by this artist into the enigmatic. There is always the hush of mystery, and often a sense of humor."[1] Although these comments were made prior to Paris' working with handmade paper they are equally valid today.

Wayfarer: the Dusk Hours Which Stands Before (1976; cat. no. 48) and *Kind Bees Consoling a Devastated Citadel* (1976; cat. no. 47) are from the artist's *Soul Carta Series* of 1975–76. The series is an extension of an earlier group of small format sculptures, entitled *Souls,* begun in 1969. The *Souls* are cast in silicone with colorants and imbedded collage elements. Paris continued to make them simultaneously with the *Soul Cartas,* which are made of pressed imbeds of pigmented pulp to which unusual forms of collage are applied. For example, real bees have been placed into the pulp of *Kind Bees Consoling a Devastated Citadel.* The term "carta" is Italian for paper.

Many of the recent cartas are done on a large scale, a factor which aids Paris in fulfilling his desire to strongly affect the spectator. Each is made through a special process that Paris developed with equipment in his own studio. Other modes include small intimate wall pieces, table pieces, and objects enclosed in boxes. In all, the sense of mystery or surprise, poetry or thought provocation, as described by Selz above, is achieved through the juxtaposition of uncommon or seemingly contradictory imagery, as well as by the literary associations of the titles. According to Paris, his work in all media has been done with the same intent, to "search for a personal vision, one that reflects often elements of fantasy that speak of a world seen as mirrors in a child's world."[2]

[1]Peter Selz, "Harold Persico Paris: The California Years," *Art International,* XVI/4, April 20, 1972, p. 56.
[2]Harold Paris, response to a questionnaire, 1977.

Bibliography

Joanne A. Dickson, "Sensing the Inner Spirit," *Artweek,* VI/21, June 14, 1975, p. 3.
Richard Kubiak, *The Handmade Paper Object,* The Santa Barbara Museum of Art, October 29–November 28, 1976.
Peter Selz, "Harold Persico Paris: The California Years," *Art International,* XVI/4, April 20, 1972, pp. 42–44, 56.

Robert Rauschenberg
b. 1925

49 *Box Cars* (from *Bones*), 1975
Handmade paper, bamboo and fabric
34 x 26½ x 3 in.
Lent by Gemini G.E.L., Los Angeles

50 *Snake Eyes* (from *Bones*), 1975
Handmade paper, bamboo and fabric
33¾ x 26¼ x 1½ in.
Lent by Gemini G.E.L., Los Angeles

51 *Ally* (from *Unions*), 1975
    Rag-mud, rope, dyed string and bamboo
    45 x 49 x 3½ in.
    Lent by Gemini G.E.L., Los Angeles

52 *Charter* (from *Unions*), 1975
    Rag-mud, rope and bamboo
    81 x 29½ x 23½ in.
    Lent by Gemini G.E.L., Los Angeles

Robert Rauschenberg's art can be characterized, in part, as a continual exploration of new
methods, materials, and ideas. In 1973 he collaborated with Gemini G.E.L. and traveled to a
four hundred year old French paper mill to be assisted by local papermakers in creating the series
known as *Pages* and *Fuses*.[1] The *Bones* and
Unions series, in the present exhibition, is the

result of a second collaboration between the artist, Gemini, and foreign craftsmen. These works were produced between May and June, 1975, at paper and textile mills of the Sarabhai family near Ahmedabad, Gujaret, India.

Both *Bones* and *Unions* were made in multiples. The *Bones* (cat. no. 49 and 50) consist of bamboo ribs and cut fabrics embedded between two pieces of wet pulp. Although fabric shapes are constant throughout each edition, no fabric appears more than once in the same position. The *Unions* are more sculptural and carry on the Rauschenberg tradition of stretching the limitations and definitions of art objects and processes. The substance from which the *Union* slabs were formed was dubbed " rag-mud" by Rauschenberg. It is a mixture of paper pulp with binding powders and spices (fenugreek and tamarind) and an adobe-like mud used by Ahmedabad Indians to build houses. The rag-mud was shaped by hand according to the artist's drawings. Once solidified the rag-mud slabs were combined with string, rope, and bamboo rods to form assemblages such as *Charter* (cat. no. 52) and *Ally* (cat. no. 51). In the latter the string and bamboo rod can be adjusted to different positions. Thus, *Ally* not only involves the use of innovative materials, but, when carefully arranged, becomes a richly textured image of subtle grace and balance.

[1] For further information on the *Pages* and *Fuses* see Richard Kubiak, *The Handmade Paper Object,* The Santa Barbara Museum of Art, October 29–November 28, 1976, n.p.

Bibliography
"Multiples and Objects and Artists' Books," *The Print Collector's Newsletter,* VI/5, November–December, 1975, p. 137.
Melinda Wortz, "Rauschenberg's 'Bones and Unions'," *Artweek,* VI/35, October 18, 1975, p. 2.

Richard Royce
b. 1941

53 *Frozen Motion Closed I,* 1977
Cast handmade paper print
17 x 17 x 16 in.
Lent by the Artist

54 *Frozen Motion Closed II,* 1977
Cast handmade paper print
17 x 17 x 16 in.
Lent by the Artist

55 *Frozen Motion Open,* 1977
Cast handmade paper print
18 x 37 x 17 in.
Lent by the Artist

56 *Traces,* 1977
Cast handmade paper
29 x 29 in.
Lent by the Artist

57 *View Through My Window,* 1977
Cast handmade paper, airbrush and ink
7 x 7 ft. x 4 in.
Lent by the Artist

The desire to synthesize his aesthetic impulses towards sculpture and printmaking led Richard Royce into involvement in what he calls the "pulp movement."[1] He notes that prior to casting with paper, "I had been struggling with several problems: How to print very high reliefs without destroying my press; how to print super large prints when limited by the size of the press (and the impossibility of commercially obtaining super large pieces of paper)…and how to develop my work with engraving and line to a monumental form."[2] The ease and flexibility of casting with pulp seemed the logical solution to these problems.

Royce's *Frozen Motion Series* (1977; cat. nos. 53–55) illustrates how he redefined the traditional notion of a print. Wet pulp was cast inside a pyramidal shaped mold, the interior of which had been carved in relief. When the pulp dried, the artist removed the mold and was left with a three-dimensional form of woodblock print.

View Through My Window (1977; cat. no. 57) seems much less like a print than Royce's other works. Here the artist used wet pulp to cast the impression of his studio window, an action that has significance on several levels. It demonstrated that one could cast almost anything in paper, on any scale, if he set his mind to it. The work can be viewed as a new approach to a traditional subject, the artist's studio. It also continues the Dada/Surrealist tradition of taking a familiar object and placing it in a new context, making the viewer aware of its inherent aesthetic qualities. Hence the impression of the studio window becomes an effective study in abstract form, as evidenced in the strong interplay among rectangular elements and in the contrast of surface textures.

[1] Richard Royce, response to a questionnaire, 1977.
[2] *Ibid.*

57 Richard Royce, *View Through My Window*, 1977

Bibliography
Gordon J. Hazlett, "Los Angeles," *Art News,*
XLLVI/5, May, 1977, pp. 104–105.
Richard Kubiak, *The Handmade Paper Object,*
The Santa Barbara Museum of Art, October 29–
November 28, 1976.
Adrienne Rosenthal, "Prints and Paper,"
Artweek, VIII/25, July 16, 1977, p. 6.

Allen Ruppersberg
b. 1944

58 *Personal Art,* 1973
Cardboard, ink and string
23 x 23 in.
Lent by Claire S. Copley Gallery, Los
Angeles

59 *Once a Day Once A Week,* 1973
Cardboard, ink and string
7 pieces, each 23 x 23 in.
Lent by Claire S. Copley Gallery, Los
Angeles

60   Allen Ruppersberg, *Ready and Waiting,* 1973

60   *Ready and Waiting,* 1973
Cardboard, ink and coathanger
23 x 23 in.
Lent by Claire S. Copley Gallery, Los
Angeles

61   *Self Portrait and Sculpture,* 1973
Cardboard and paper
9 x 11½ x 16 in.
Lent by Claire S. Copley Gallery, Los
Angeles

Allen Ruppersberg sees two factors as being
consistent throughout his art: his work is always
very personal and he employs common materials.[1] Both concerns are evident in the cardboard
cut-out pieces which Ruppersberg made in 1973.
Using as a guide a cut-out of his profile, traced by
an assistant while the artist sat before a projector,
Ruppersberg proceeded to cut his profile out of
single and multiple slabs of simple cardboard,
leaving the resulting negative space to assume
the form of his image. Handwritten inscriptions
across the cardboard surfaces give specific
meaning to each work. *Personal Art* (cat. no. 58)
best describes the intention of the series, while
Ready and Waiting (cat. no. 60) pertains to a particular state which the artist experiences from
time to time—the period of lapse in productivity,
of not doing anything. The coat hanger from
which this piece is suspended, then, appears to
function as a visual pun—a means of stating the
idea of the artist "hanging" in anticipation of the
next phase in his life or career. *Once a Day Once
a Week* (cat. no. 59) consists of seven slabs, each
inscribed with a different day of the week. *Self-
Portrait and Sculpture* (cat. no. 61) is a box which
sits on the floor, and utilizes the greatest amount
of negative space to signify the artist's portrait.
This work was the last in the series, and was
made by a printer according to Ruppersberg's
specifications. The artist left his profile cut-out
with the printer and instructed him to stack to the
brim the interior of a standard cardboard carton
with several pieces of ordinary typing paper
in which the profile had been cut out. The climac-
tic aspect of the project is that Ruppersberg
requested the box be delivered to him sealed.
Only when he opened the box to reveal his own
image was the work complete.

[1] Allen Ruppersberg, phone conversation with
David S. Rubin, September 26, 1977.

Ursula Schneider
b. 1943

62   *Here I Am No. 1,* 1977
Painted paper coated with wax
32 x 26 in.
Lent by Braunstein/Quay Gallery, San Francisco

63   *Here I Am No. 3,* 1977
Painted paper coated with wax
32 x 26 in.
Lent by Braunstein/Quay Gallery, San Francisco

64   *Here I Am No. 4,* 1977
Painted paper coated with wax
32 x 26 in.
Lent by Braunstein/Quay Gallery, San Francisco

65   *Here I Am No. 5,* 1977
Painted paper coated with wax
32 x 26 in.
Lent by Braunstein/Quay Gallery, San Francisco

66   *Here I Am No. 6,* 1977
Painted paper coated with wax
32 x 26 in.
Lent by Braunstein/Quay Gallery, San Francisco

The sculpture of Ursula Schneider involves a
continual exploration of new materials to express
some inner meaning. In 1974 she used woven
vinyl to build haunting images of large insects and
winged creatures.[1] Her death masks of 1976

were made entirely from human hair.[2] By no means limiting herself to working with a single material, the artist found a use for paper in 1977—making from it sculptures which have a personal, autobiographical content.

The *Here I Am Series* (cat. nos. 62–66) was made from paper pieces which were painted on both sides, and then coated with hot wax. The result is a group of conical sculptures which are meant to stand in an arrangement that recalls *Stonehenge.* Each is different in color and surface pattern. While some are soft and lyrical, others are bright with jagged edges. Schneider considers each cone to represent different aspects of her psychological make-up. She refers

to the series as "an exploration of my states of being. In an attempt to order them, I found them related to past and present, transitory, only to be experienced one at a time, as a point of view, screening perception."[3]

[1] For descriptions of these works see Alan Meisel, "San Francisco," *Craft Horizons,* XXXIV/4, August, 1974, p. 34 and Jerome Tarshis, "When Cultures Collide," *Art News,* LXXIII/7, September, 1974, p. 80.
[2] Peter Frank, "Ursula Schneider," *Art News,* LXXV/10, December, 1976, p. 116.
[3] Ursula Schneider, response to a questionnaire, 1977.

David Smith
b. 1943

67 *Untitled,* 1976
Handmade paper
67 x 81 in.
Lent by Jean and Morton Beckner, Claremont

68 *Untitled,* 1976
Handmade paper
52 x 44¼ in.
Lent by the Artist

Playboy Magazine and H. W. Janson's *History of Art,* two seemingly unrelated publications, were joined together in an untitled work by David Smith (1976; cat. no. 68). The grayish tones were made by mixing into the wet pulp small fragments of *Playboy* centerfolds, while the lighter zone used bits and pieces of the standard art history text. In this fashion, Smith found a way to reconcile literary content and formalist abstraction within a single image.

Earlier Smith had been making wax paper constructions. Seeking to enlarge the scale of his works, he experimented with ordinary blenders and a large fiberglass screen with homemade wooden frame and manufactured his own paper. The original idea was to have a message of written words lie within the paper rather than on the surface. Yet in the early examples, small pieces of paper with recognizable phrases were collaged on to the surface. This collage element was soon abandoned when the artist realized that the content came from the choice of the material itself.

The compositional structures of the works were carefully controlled by the artist as he manipulated the pulp by hand on the large screen. In *Untitled* (cat. no. 68) Smith explored edge relationships, color contrasts, and the interaction between open and closed spaces.

Keith Sonnier
b. 1941

69 *C-IX* (from *Abaca-Code Series*), 1976
Cast handmade paper, hand stamped
6½ x 6½ ft.
Lent by Gemini G.E.L., Los Angeles

70 *R-VII,* (from *Abaca-Code Series*), 1976
Cast handmade paper, hand stamped
6 x 8 ft.
Lent by Gemini G.E.L., Los Angeles

Although Keith Sonnier has worked in several different media, there is a factor which remains constant throughout his *oeuvre*: it is his particular visual language of the circle, the rectangle, and the square. This geometric vocabulary was introduced in Sonnier's glass sculptures of 1968 and is also seen in his videoscreened images of the early 1970s.[1] Bruce Kurtz characterized Sonnier's art in 1973 as a "definition of the interrelationships of color, surface, space, and material...in his latex and flocking pieces, gauze and flocking pieces, neon and glass pieces, films, per-

formances, live video pieces and video tapes. In all of these works, surface as an integral aspect of colored material located in space is a primary consideration."[2]

Seen in perspective, then, the *Abaca-Code Series* continues Sonnier's exploration of surface and shape relationships using a specific and limited pictorial vocabulary. The large handmade paper pieces are divided into three groups according to the shape of the field: circular, rectangular, or square. Within each group is a calculated system of shape and color patterns. For example, the circles (cat. no. 69) all share the same arrangement of interior shapes, but differ in number (*C-I, C-II, C-III,* etc.) and color; for each color combination there is a twin example where the colors of the field and imagery have been reversed.

Sonnier initiated the project in September, 1975. He approached Gemini G.E.L. with the idea

of making large paper pieces through a collaborative effort. After considerable research and experimentation by the participants in the project, a system evolved where, on a large table, pulp was poured within the perimeters of a rectangular, circular, or square shape deckle (of 8 to 10 feet in length). Smaller molds were used for interior shapes; colors were determined by the color of the rags ground into the pulp. Due to the large size of the pieces, excess water had to be removed with a vacuum. For drying them, a make-shift oven was formed by sectioning off the corner of a room which was directly connected to the heating system. The lettering of each work was done by inking large metal stamps, tooled to the artist's specifications, and pounding them onto the surface with a sledge hammer. Each example was stamp dated 1976 (in Roman numerals) as the series was completed in February of that year.

[1] See Robert Pincus-Witten, "Keith Sonnier: Video and Film as Color-Field," *Artforum,* X/9, May, 1972, pp. 35–37.

[2] Bruce Kurtz, "Video is Being Invented," *Arts Magazine,* XLVII/3, December–January, 1973, p. 38.

Bibliography
Suzanne Boorsch, "New Editions,"*Art News,* LXXV/3, March, 1976, p. 68.

Lenders

ADI Gallery, San Francisco
The Allrich Gallery, San Francisco
John Babcock, Santa Maria, California
Jean and Morton Beckner, Claremont
Braunstein/Quay Gallery, San Francisco
Susan Caldwell Gallery, New York City
Cirrus Gallery, Los Angeles
Claire S. Copley Gallery, Los Angeles
Dominic L. Di Mare, Tiburon, California
David and Cloyce Flaten, La Verne, California
Gemini G.E.L., Los Angeles
Harrison Gill, Santa Maria, California
Grapestake Gallery, San Francisco
Charles Christopher Hill, Los Angeles
Karen Laubhan, Santa Cruz
Richard Royce, Santa Monica
William Sawyer Gallery, San Francisco
Smith Andersen Gallery, Palo Alto
David Smith, New York City
Vanguard Gallery, Los Angeles

Staff of the Galleries of the Claremont Colleges

David W. Steadman, Director
David S. Rubin, Assistant Director
Kay Koeninger Warren, Registrar
Charmaine Soldat, Galleries Coordinator
Doug Humble, Galleries Manager

Photography Credits

F. L. Avery, Santa Cruz (cat. no. 32)
Jeremiah O. Bragstad, San Francisco (cat. no. 18)
Neil Fenn, Los Angeles (cat. nos. 5, 38, 68)
Charles Christopher Hill, Los Angeles (cat. no. 23)
Gary Krueger, Los Angeles (cat. no. 60)